I0753531

FINISHING LINE PRESS
www.finishinglinepress.com

Morocco

Poems and Photographs
by

John Delaney

Finishing Line Press
Georgetown, Kentucky

Morocco

ISBN 979-8-89990-365-6 First Edition

Publisher: Leah Huete de Maines
Editor: Christen Kincaid
Cover art and photographs: John Delaney
Author photo: Susan Delaney
Cover design: John Delaney

Order online: www.finishinglinepress.com
also available on amazon.com

Author inquiries and mail orders:
Finishing Line Press
PO Box 1626
Georgetown, Kentucky 40324
USA

Contents

View of fertile valley on the way to the archaeolgical site of the Roman city of Volubilis

Traveling leaves you speechless, then turns you into a storyteller.
—Ibn Battuta (1304-1369), Moroccan-born Muslim traveler of 75,000 miles, the most of anyone known before the modern era

Carpets

Moroccan magic, woven in the rug,
elicits from the cat a kind of whimsy.
He throws himself down and rolls around
ecstatically, as if it were catnip.

Called "Sand Dunes," waves of vibrant colors weave
through the runner. Their patterns ripple
like winds moving dunes across the Sahara,
grain by grain, sand powdered in the sun.

I imagine the weaver in her village home,
during the many months she worked on this,
was imagining, too, rolling in dunes
as a youth again, turning the seconds over.

From loom to room, the mind rides a magic carpet.

Every rug has a story. Bought in Marrakesh, this contemporary Berber rug is made from wool and vegetable dyes. It comes from a village in the "high" region of the Atlas Mountains.

21

Doors

Each door is the final arbiter.
State your reason for entering.
Knock, knock. Or unlock.

Ornate. Detailed. But windowless.
Does it boast of inside splendor?
Belie embarrassed squalor?

Deadbolt your private paradise.
Guard possessions from the prying world.
Shutout noise behind.

Pull the handle for your friends.
Grasp the knob worn out by family members.
Turn the key to your home.

Open or closed. Entranceway or exit.
These stalwart umpires make the call—
'welcome' or 'goodbye'—for all.

Moroccan doors are known for their hand-carved details and intricately tiled doorways.

The Sahara Farmer

Literally divined by a Y-shaped rod,
the farm was established by his father.
It has succeeded now for forty years,
two wells supplying all needed water.

We followed the kaftan-wearing farmer
past irrigated plots of alfalfa,
garlic, and onions, towards an impressive
grove of date palm trees, his best cash crop.

He demonstrated how he pollinates
each female tree himself, clambering up
the bark in his sandals. Spry and limber
at sixty-seven, he made short shrift of it.

He teased us to identify the seeds
of henna he held as we walked back through
football fields of farmland framed by dunes.
Everything was lush and green, ripening

in a practical patch of paradise.
Who knew what one could cultivate from sand?
Who would guess they were in the Sahara?
Where there's a will, there's a way. Praise Allah.

Agriculture is a dominant economic sector in Morocco and employs about one-third of its workforce.

Medinas

Only a resident would know the way
through the narrow, winding, walled medina.
That would keep strangers and the riff-raff out.
But not the cats, those navigating souls
that follow their own track—what we call knack.

We took the dare and explored on our own.
We found stalls and shops and residences,
some alleys as dark and quiet as caves.
From a rooftop restaurant, we observed
(and heard) a tradesman crafting copper pots

in a small square filled with foreign tourists.
If being lost means everything seems strange
and new, we were lost. When a gate appeared,
we emerged into city streets and traffic.
We hadn't been bidden, but went back in.

In Morocco, a medina is the original, old, walled part of the city, usually car-less because of the narrow alleyways.

38390 ب 6

Cats

Given nine lives, cats have much too much time
on their hands and donate lots to snoozing—
on a motorcycle seat, on the hood
of a car, in the weedy undergrowth
of a sidewalk tree, lost among sneakers.
Anytime, anywhere, they're sleep seekers.

Their cleanliness is next to godliness,
devoting themselves daily to their prayers.
Nimble, spry, they always land on their feet.
When opportunity appears, they pounce.
Everything is potentially play
to them, and night is just another day.

They remind us to keep things in focus
and not succumb to life's hocus-pocus.
Plaintive meows bespeak their royalty,
inviting us to share their wide worldview.
With a piercing stare, they even dare you:
'Are you willing and able to love me?'

Revered in Islam, cats are admired for their cleanliness and allowed to enter homes and mosques freely. They are to be well-cared for, treasured, and loved. The Prophet Mohammed was devoted to felines.

Volubilis

You pass through the gate as through a time warp
of centuries into a Roman world
of streets and homes and businesses.
There is much that remains in this rubble
still overlooking a fine fertile valley.

You imagine the lives of the people,
taking their families to the public baths
fed by an aqueduct from the mountains.
Squeezing olives at the co-op, inviting
friends over to marvel at the new mosaic floor.

They imagined things, too. Elephants and tigers,
gods and goddesses are depicted there.
The towering columns support stork nests now.
A colonnaded street reminds you of processions
with banners flying, honoring each passing year.

Anyway, you could have been happy here.

One of Morocco's best-preserved Roman ruins located near Meknes above a fertile plain surrounded by wheat fields. Founded in the 3rd century B.C, Volubilis, at its peak in the 2nd century A.D., is thought to have had 20,000 residents. It is a UNESCO World Heritage Site.

Hassan II Mosque, Casablanca

Here is a place large enough to hold
the prayers of 25,000 Muslims.
It overhangs the water which, the Quran says,
bears god's throne. His waves roll underneath
in a ceaseless cleansing ritual.

Here is a place 6000 artisans wrought
from fragrant cedar wood and pink granite.
Intricate marble flooring and inlay,
gilded ceilings and exquisite zellige
(geometric mosaic tilework) abound.

Here is a place ordained by a king.
Its gates formed from brass and titanium.
Its ablution stations in the basement,
carved from local marble, ease water
through their lotus-shaped designs.

Here is a place that lasers on Mecca
from a sixty-story minaret.
Its retractable roof invites sunlight
and starlight to highlight the worshippers.
It's the stronghold of a country's faith.

Hassan II Mosque in Casablanca is the largest functioning mosque in Africa and the seventh largest in the world. It is the most ambitious structure ever built in Morocco and can house 25,000 worshippers inside and 80,000 more in its courtyards.

Souks

The stalls are approachable.
The goods are promotional.
The customers are sociable.
Venders are knowledgeable.

So, every day's remarkable,
For everything's negotiable.

Souks are traditional marketplace districts found throughout Morocco consisting of stalls offering a wide array of goods, from exquisite woodwork and lighting fixtures to basic food, spices, and even herbal remedies.

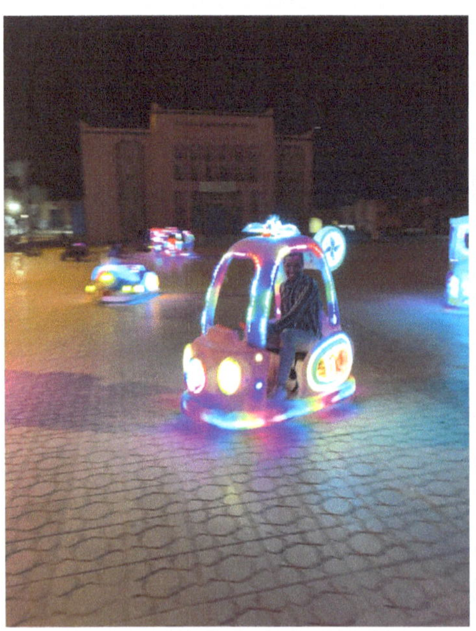

Riding Kiddie Cars in Quarzazate

Where's-is-at is the best we could do
pronouncing this place near where films were made.
Returning at night from a restaurant
close to our hotel, we reached the main square
and found brightly-lit electric kiddie cars!
Who were they kidding? Of course we would try
to be kids again, and that's what we did,
responding to loud music from Disney.

I rode a dolphin and finned through the ocean,
passing a jaunty jeep with glowing tires,
a heedless horse-drawn carriage, a runaway
locomotive bearing down with bright lights.
We were wild drivers and sped about.
Too soon we timed out.

Quarzazate is known as the gateway to the Sahara Desert as well as the region of Morocco's film industry. Atlas Studios is the largest (by land area) film studio in the world; many well-known international movies have had scenes shot there.

Nomads

They've lived off the grid for twenty years,
raising children and a small herd of sheep.
Reliable water's a mile away,
carted back in yellow plastic drums.
They save an empty tent for their chickens
and a pen to keep the sheep safe at night.
There's a washing hut and a baking tent.

Did I say how practical their life is
in these low mountains? Winter's a playground
for sledders on the open snowy slopes.
They watch over unhindered horizon.
Far removed from the town's teeming markets
and the city's bright distractions, at night
their dreams ride on handmade Berber carpets.

There are about 25,000 nomads living in Morocco, even in desert areas, but their numbers are dwindling sharply due to the intense droughts of climate change.

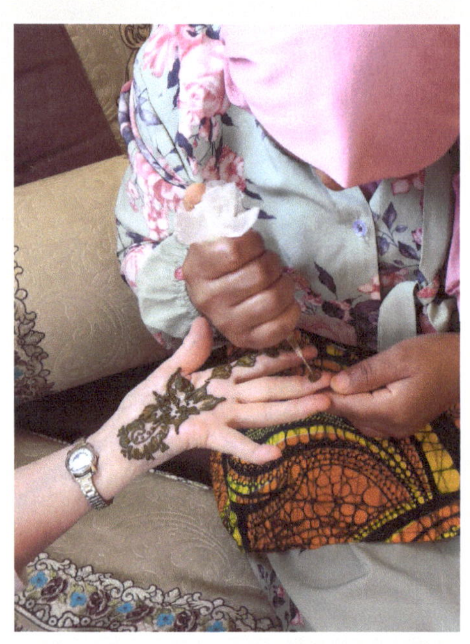

Henna

The process of this tattoo-making
requires a steady hand, unshaking,
so a continuous line can be laid
down by the needle's glass blade.

Precisely like a surgeon's scalpel,
but above the skin,
this moving line will begin
almost feeling palpable

of the practitioner's art:
she, who draws from imagination
and a flowering heart
a unique creation.

The brown dye stain that remains
gradually fades away in shades
like a lingering memory.

In Morocco, henna tattoos are most common on the hands and feet. They are thought to bring good luck.

Buying a Leather Jacket in Fez

Stone vats of colored dyes and white liquids.
Hides of cows, sheep, goats, and camels.
The eager salesman explained the process,
how they need to soak for two or three days
among cow urine and pigeon feces
to clean and soften the skins for the dyes,
natural colorants like indigo
and henna and poppy. Then they are dried
in the sun. Craftsmen create the products
by hand—slippers and handbags and jackets—
using methods from the Middle Ages.

Of course, their products were special, he said.
To prove the point, he lit a matchbook flame
and held it up against the supple leather
that surprisingly seemed flame retardant.
Which leads me to think there's no reason why
I can't safely stride through a raging fire.

Well, at least it should keep me warm and dry.

Fez (or Fes), the second largest city in Morocco, has been called the "Athens of Africa" and is considered the spiritual and cultural capital of the country.

Riad

Riads

Down a nondescript passageway in the medina,
literally off the beaten track,
an ornamental wooden door beckons
and calls you back.
Inside—surprise—a hidden palace of rooms
surrounding an open-air courtyard and fountain
where tranquility blooms and perfumes.
Exquisite mosaics and woodwork
decorate the floors and ceilings,
plush fabrics and furnishings the space.

A reprieve from the marketplace
of rhythmic ruckus and sensuous sights.
You can sit here sheltered in your own thoughts.
Call it home for a few nights.

A Riad is a traditional Moroccan house or palace with an indoor garden and courtyard located within the old city. Once the residences of wealthy citizens, they are now boutique hotels.

Roaming Around Rabat

A city of white in the brilliant sun,
oceanside, along the Bou Regreg River.
We taxied in from the airport, driving past
the curving Grand Theatre, like a swirl
of calligraphy, and the gherkin-shaped
business tower, named after the king.

Our riad hid deep in the medina,
so we followed a guide with our bags
and later learned to navigate the maze
to new surprises round every corner.
Shops and souks and uniformed children.
A box of kittens with a bowl of water.

Walled Chellah's ancient Roman ruins
now house storks and cats, but at Bab Zadr,
the main gate, a snazzily-dressed musician
drummed away the time to entertain us.
We had lunch along the river and watched
a woman in hijab feeding pigeons.

We caught the changing of the horse guard
at Hassan Tower and mausoleum.
And through the Kasbah of the Oudyas,
a citadel of cafes and garden grounds,
one of our afternoons sauntered and strolled.
Somehow we stumbled on embassy row.

Artifacts of the country's history,
bronzes and sculptures in the main museum,
vouched for the march of civilization.
It never seemed to stop, the work I mean
of the ubiquitous brush-broom sweepers,
at the king's request, keeping the streets clean.

Rabat is the capital of Morocco, known as the Royal City since it is the seat of the Royal family—also the Washington of North Africa for its parks, boulevards, embassies, and government buildings. [Street sweeper photograph taken by Susan Delaney.]

The Fossil Shop

It's the age, right, that fascinates people
about fossils? Holding something sooo old
in our hands? Marveling at what once was?

That something exceptional has come and gone
on this planet, making us possible,
so to speak, having tested the waters
and finding them usable, suitable.
And the compulsive progression of it all,
each turn of a shell, say, enlarging on the other,
over hundreds of millions of years.
A poignant record of reckoning
the tough elements with implacable patience.

Earth's cremains: we draft them for a table,
a shelf knickknack, a conversation piece.

Morocco is one of the world's largest sources for fossils due to the Sahara Desert and the ocean that once covered it. As a result, the fossil trade is booming, and some worry that the scale of it is damaging the country's paleontological heritage.

EARTH
CAFE

HENNA
ART CAFE

Marrakesh

You expect a carnival and you get one:
snake charmers and small bellhop-dressed monkeys.
The main plaza seemed to spin in circles.
I got a beer in a square-side bar
with a full view of the activity,
and a young man dressed like a sheik set up
his mic and speaker, then plugged in his guitar
and started playing English pop songs,
like Sheeran's "Bad Habits" and "Perfect".
Then he packed his things up and moved next door.

Most tourists take a tour of Bahia Palace
or Le Jardin Secret or the lush home
where Yves Saint Laurent once lived
in extraordinary splendor and color.
We even took a balloon ride outside
the city to catch the sun rise over
the mountains. I bought a lovely carpet
and paid a craftsman to etch my cat's name
on a tile with his profile. Yes, busker,
'Marrakesh is bad habits and perfect.'

Marrakesh is the fourth largest city in Morocco, and its major square is the busiest in all of Africa. Its medina quarter is a UNESCO World Heritage Site.

A Souvenir of Sand

How to get familiar with infinity . . .
A camel ride into the Sahara
to stargaze a wide open desert sky?

The astronomer Carl Sagan once said
stars outnumbered grains of sand on beaches—
so I rode a camel from Merzouga

out into oceanic dunes of sand
and sat there after sunset for the stars,
dwelling for a time with two infinities,

it seemed, or was it two eternities?
I felt *forever* in the sandy dust
flowing like a fountain through my fingers.

I found endless sand and stars to ooh and ah.
Beholding leads to praying. Inshallah.

The Sahara's surface of sand measures approximately 3.5 million square miles, the size of the contiguous U.S. Washed by the wind rather than water, its fine grains are unsuitable for making concrete.

Aït Benhaddou is an historic fortified village in Morocco on the old caravan route between the Sahara and Marrakesh. Few families live in it now. A UNESCO World Heritage Site since 1987, it has been featured in many international films.

Acknowledgments

Grateful appreciation is due the editors of the following magazines where these poems and photographs first appeared:

Alternate Route: "The Fossil Shop", "Marrakesh", "Riding Kiddie Cars in Quarzazate" (with color photographs)

Deep Overstock: "Buying a Leather Jacket in Fez", "Henna", "A Souvenir of Sand" (with color photographs)

Last Leaves: "Volubilis" (with color photograph)

Mediterranean Poetry: "Doors", "Hassan II Mosque, Casablanca", "Medinas" "Nomads", "Roaming Around Rabat", "Riads", "The Sahara Farmer", "Souks" (with color photographs)

October Hill Magazine: "Cats"

Young Ravens Literary Review: "Carpets" (with color photograph)

Children singing Morocco's national anthem

John Delaney retired after 35 years in the Dept. of Rare Books and Special Collections of Princeton University Library, where he was head of manuscripts processing and then, for his last 15 years, also curator of historic maps. He has written a number of works on cartography, including *Strait Through: Magellan to Cook and the Pacific; First X, Then Y, Now Z: An Introduction to Landmark Thematic Maps;* and *Nova Caesarea: A Cartographic Record of the Garden State, 1666-1888.* These have extensive website versions.

He has written poems for most of his life, and, in the 1970s, he attended the Writing Program of Syracuse University, where his mentors were poets W. D. Snodgrass and Philip Booth. No doubt, in subtle ways, they have bookended his approach to poems. His publications include *Waypoints* (2017), a collection of place poems, Twenty Questions (2019), a chapbook, Delicate Arch (2022), poems and photographs of national parks and monuments, Galápagos (2023), a collaborative chapbook of his son Andrew's photographs and his poems, *Nile* (2024), a chapbook of poems and photographs about Egypt, *Filing Order: Sonnets* (2025), and *CATechisms* (2025), poems and photographs about his senior cat, Ramen. He lives in Port Townsend, WA.

About This Book

The result of an extended trip to Morocco John took with his sister Susan in 2023, *Morocco* examines the everyday culture and prominent sites of the country with poems inspired by photographs. Whether it's getting lost in the alleyways of a medina, enjoying the marketplace of souks and the grandeur of riads, following the footsteps of the Romans, learning of the life of nomads and Sahara farmers, exploring the attractions of Casablanca and Marrakesh, experiencing henna art and leather and carpet production, finding fondness for ubiquitous cats—all are subjects for reflection and personal growth.

www.ingramcontent.com/pod-product-compliance
Lightning Source LLC
LaVergne TN
LVHW052310100826
845147LV00006B/722

* 9 7 9 8 8 9 9 9 0 3 6 5 6 *